W9-CLB-966

LIGHTNING BOLT BOOKS

Hero Therapy Dogs

Jon M. Fishman

Lerner Publications • Minneapolis

For my therapy dog, Kaya—J. M. F.

Lerner Publications Company
A division of Lerner Publishing Group, Inc.
241 First Avenue North
Minneapolis, MN 55401 USA

For reading levels and more information, look up this title at www.lernerbooks.com.

Library of Congress Cataloging-in-Publication Data

Names: Fishman, Jon M., author.
Title: Hero therapy dogs / Jon M. Fishman.
Description: Minneapolis : Lerner Publications, [2017] | Series: Lightning bolt books™. Hero dogs | Audience: Age 5–8. | Audience: Grade K to Grade 3. | Includes bibliographical references and index.
Identifiers: LCCN 2016018649 (print) | LCCN 2016023220 (ebook) | ISBN 9781512425406 (lb : alk. paper) | ISBN 9781512431117 (pb : alk. paper) | ISBN 9781512428032 (eb pdf)
Subjects: LCSH: Dogs—Therapeutic use. | Human-animal relationships.
Classification: LCC RM931.D63 F57 2017 (print) | LCC RM931.D63 (ebook) | DDC 615.8/5158—dc23

LC record available at https://lccn.loc.gov/2016018649

Manufactured in the United States of America
1-41308-23252-4/21/2016

Table of Contents

Hospital Dogs

Is that a tail wagging? Who is walking down the hospital hallway? It's a therapy dog!

This service dog is helping its owner cross the street.

Therapy dogs are different from service dogs. A service dog is trained to do a specific job. A therapy dog gives comfort.

At a hospital, therapy dogs spend time with patients. They help patients feel calmer and happier.

Therapy dogs are for petting!

Some hospital patients have dogs at home. They miss their furry friends. Petting a therapy dog could make them feel better.

Some hospitals allow therapy dogs and their handlers to visit almost any patient. At other hospitals, a handler must get a doctor's okay before visiting a patient.

Doctors know which patients feel well enough for a dog visit.

Handlers keep therapy dogs clean. But they also put a towel under the dog to be extra safe.

A therapy dog may lie in bed with a patient. The handler puts a towel under the dog to keep the bed clean.

Handlers train therapy dogs to be calm and friendly. A therapy dog must always obey its handler.

Some hospital rooms have machines. The machines help heal the patients. Therapy dogs are careful not to get in the way of anything in the room.

School Dogs

Have you ever wished you could bring your dog to school? It's probably against the rules. But maybe another dog will be at school to help you learn!

Therapy dogs are trained to sit quietly at schools.

Therapy dogs and their handlers visit schools to help students read. Some students would rather read to a dog than to a person.

Therapy dogs are patient while students read. The dogs don't laugh if students get stuck.

Therapy dogs also visit colleges. College students may feel stress. Petting a therapy dog can help!

Therapy dogs can feel stress too. At schools, dogs take breaks away from students. Therapy dogs need a quiet place to rest.

Support Dogs

This patient is healing from an injury. The therapy dog is helping!

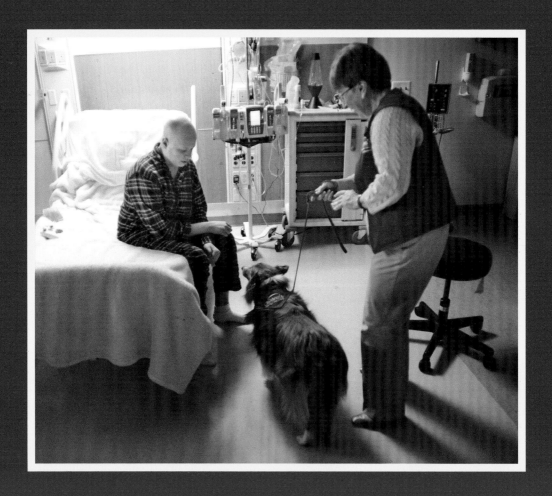

After an injury, people may need physical therapy. They must exercise to get better. A therapy dog helps to get them moving.

This dog is ready for a walk. Let's go!

Some patients want to stay in bed when they don't feel well. But they may get up to pet a therapy dog.

Therapy dogs help patients relax. Some patients feel better talking to dogs than to doctors.

Other patients have a mental illness. Therapy dogs help them feel better.

Therapy dogs must stay calm all the time.

They can't be scared by wheelchairs or loud noises.

Hospitals can be full of activity. This dog is staying cool and calm.

This dog is learning to obey its handler.

Therapy dogs know basic commands. They sit and stay. They come when their handler tells them to.

Disaster Dogs

This therapy dog travels to disaster sites. It goes where it's most needed!

This house was destroyed by a tornado.

Disasters such as tornadoes strike with little warning. Therapy dogs can help people feel better after a disaster.

Therapy dogs may remind people of happier times. Dogs are good for petting when you feel sad.

Rescue workers often travel far from home to help during disasters. These workers can also find comfort in therapy dogs.

Therapy dogs help rescue workers too.

Any kind of dog can be a therapy dog. It just needs to be friendly and well trained.

The most playful puppies will make good therapy dogs when they grow up. They are easier to train.

Therapy dogs keep people
calm. They help people heal.
Therapy dogs are heroes!

History of Therapy Dogs

Dogs have been comforting humans for hundreds of years.

- The US government first used therapy dogs during World War II (1939–1945).

- The first therapy dog's name was Smoky. Smoky helped comfort injured soldiers.

Smoky was a Yorkshire terrier.

Top Dog

Ricochet is a therapy dog. She's also a surfing dog! She hits the waves with injured soldiers. She surfs with children who have special needs.

Ricochet helps people feel better. She makes them feel as if they can do anything. Ricochet is a surfing dog hero!

Glossary

college: school after high school

command: an order a handler gives to a dog

handler: a person who takes care of and controls a therapy dog

heal: return to feeling healthy

injury: the damage from when someone gets hurt

mental illness: a medical problem that affects a patient's mood and thinking

patient: a person at a hospital to receive care

physical therapy: exercises used to treat a physical injury

stress: feelings of worry

Further Reading

Boothroyd, Jennifer. *Hero Service Dogs*. Minneapolis: Lerner Publications, 2017.

Cuddy, Robbin. *Learn to Draw Dogs & Puppies: Step-by-Step Instructions for More Than 25 Different Breeds*. Irvine, CA: Walter Foster, 2015.

Goldish, Meish. *R.E.A.D. Dogs*. New York: Bearport, 2015.

Pet Partners
https://petpartners.org

Surf Dog Ricochet the SURFice Dog
http://www.surfdogricochet.com

Therapy Dog Program—American Kennel Club
http://www.akc.org/events/title-recognition-program/therapy

Index

Photo Acknowledgments

The images in this book are used with the permission of: © iStockphoto.com/grass-lifeisgood, p. 2; © ZUMA Press Inc/Alamy, pp. 4, 9, 12, 16; © iStockphoto.com/Lokibaho, p. 5; © iStockphoto.com/monkeybusinessimages, pp. 6, 7; Douglas R. Clifford/ZUMAPRESS/Newscom, p. 8; AP Photo/Rockford Register Star, Amy J. Correnti, p. 10; AP Photo/The Abilene Reporter-News, Nellie Doneva, p. 11; © Jamie Hooper/Shutterstock.com, p. 13; AP Photo/Corpus Christi Caller-Times, Rachel Denny Clow, p. 14; © Igorr/Dreamstime.com, p. 15; © H. Mark Weidman Photography/Alamy, p. 17; © 67photo/Alamy, p. 18; © iStockphoto.com/jeangill, p. 19; © The Washington Post/Getty Images, p. 20; © iStockphoto.com/knape, p. 21; © iStockphoto.com/sengulmurat, p. 22; © Benjamin Simeneta/Dreamstime.com, p. 23; © LaKirr/Shutterstock.com, p. 24; AP Photo/Elaine Thompson, p. 25; © iStockphoto.com/AnetaPics, pp. 26, 30; © Chris Jackson/Staff/Getty Images, p. 27; Courtesy of Smoky War Dog LLC, p. 28.

Front cover: © iStockphoto.com/CreativaImages.

Main body text set in Billy Infant regular 28/36. Typeface provided by SparkType.